COUNTRIES IN OUR WORLD

FRANCE
IN OUR WORLD

Camilla de la Bédoyère

A+

Smart Apple Media

Published by Smart Apple Media
P.O. Box 3263, Mankato, Minnesota 56002

Printed in the United States of America by Corporate
Graphics, North Mankato, Minnesota.

Published by arrangement with the Watts Publishing
Group Ltd., London.

Library of Congress Cataloging-in-Publication Data

de la Bédoyère, Camilla.
  France in our world / by Camilla de la Bédoyère.
     p. cm. -- (Countries in our world)
  Includes index.
  Summary: "Describes the economy, government,
and culture of France today and discusses France's
influence of and relations with the rest of the world"
--Provided by publisher.
  ISBN 978-1-59920-437-6 (library binding)
  1. France--Juvenile literature. I. Title.
  DC17.D4 2010
  944--dc22

                              2009031770

1207
32010

9 8 7 6 5 4 3 2 1

Produced by: White-Thomson Publishing Ltd.

Series consultant: Rob Bowden
Editor: Sonya Newland
Designer: Alix Wood
Picture researcher: Amy Sparks

Picture Credits
Corbis: Cover (Tim de Waele), 13 (Philippe Giraud/
Goodlook Pictures), 14 (Philippe Lissac/Godong),
16 (epa), 20 (Owen Franken), 22 (G. Bowater),
28 (Philippe Giraud/Goodlook); **Fotolia:** 11 (Pascal
Arnaud), 12 (Laurent Davaine); **Photoshot:** 6 (World
Pictures), 15 (Wiktor Dabkowski), 24 (Face to
Face/UPPA), 26 (UPPA), 27 (Vic Hinterlang/ WPN),
29 (Xinhua/ Landov); **Shutterstock:** 5 (Michael
Stokes), 7 (Jorge Felix Costa), 8 (Dubassy), 9 (Roca),
10 (Nola Rin), 17 (Natalia Bratslavsky), 18 (Keith
Levit), 19 (Marc Pagani Photography), 21 (Robert Paul
Van Beets), 23 (Witchcraft), 25 (Gueorgui Ianakiev).

Contents

France has been a global leader for centuries, and it once controlled one of the largest empires on Earth. Today, it is still one of the most influential countries in Europe and the world.

Where in the World?

France lies in northwest Europe and is the largest European country after Russia and Ukraine. The nation's capital city is Paris, known as *ville lumière* ("city of light"). There are French territories around the world, including Guadeloupe and Martinique in the West Indies, which are places that are partly controlled by the French government.

▲ *France shares borders with Belgium, Luxembourg, Germany, Switzerland, Italy, Andorra, and Spain and is linked to the United Kingdom by the Channel Tunnel.*

An Ancient Country

France is an old country—people have been living there for at least 35,000 years. Nearly 3,000 years ago, tribes near the Mediterranean Sea were trading with their neighbors and the seafaring Greeks. Around 2,000 years ago, Julius Caesar led his Roman troops across Europe and successfully invaded the region, which was then known as Gaul. Since those early times, France has faced wars and invasions. It has also colonized lands far beyond its borders, including parts of Africa, Asia, and the Pacific.

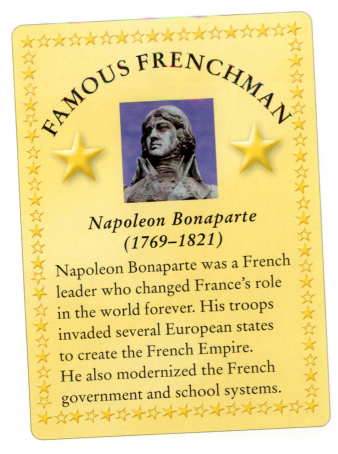

FAMOUS FRENCHMAN

Napoleon Bonaparte (1769–1821)

Napoleon Bonaparte was a French leader who changed France's role in the world forever. His troops invaded several European states to create the French Empire. He also modernized the French government and school systems.

▲ *Napoleon was defeated by the British army in 1815 at the Battle of Waterloo.*

Revolution to Republic

In the 1780s, the French people rebelled against their monarch, King Louis XVI, and this led to the French Revolution in 1789. The country was declared a republic, which means that the head of state is a president elected by the people, rather than a king or queen. Today, France has a president and a prime minister who both lead the government.

A World Power

France's position in the middle of Europe means that it acts as a link between northern and southern parts of the continent, as well as between Britain and mainland Europe. It is a member of several important international organizations, including the North Atlantic Treaty Organization (NATO), which allows certain countries—including the United States—to work together in times of conflict. France was also one of the founding members of the European Union (EU), an organization that helps European nations to trade with one another and to cooperate to avoid war.

Dom-Toms

From the sixteenth to the nineteenth centuries, many European countries sent explorers and soldiers around the world in search of new lands and riches. Like Spain and Britain, France built an empire that reached into all the corners of the globe. Many of the places France used to control are now independent, but the French government still plays a part in the way some of them are run. The French call these former colonies Dom-Toms, or Overseas Departments and Territories.

▶ *Children enjoying a carnival in the French Overseas Territory of Martinique. They have painted oars in different flag colors—the blue, white, and red oar represents the French flag.*

IT STARTED HERE

Parachutes

Jumping out of a tree clutching two umbrellas is not normally a good idea, but in 1783 it was the only way Frenchman Louis-Sébastien Lenormand could discover whether a parachute might work. The experiment was a success—Lenormand proved that he could slow his fall by increasing air resistance. Before long, other Frenchmen were jumping from great heights with parachutes made of silk or canvas.

BASIC DATA

Official name: **French Republic**

Capital: **Paris**

Size: **211,210 sq miles (547,030 sq km)**

Population: **64,057,792 (2009 est.)**

Currency: **Euro**

Beyond Borders

In the past, France's influence stretched beyond its own borders as French people took their traditions and language to other countries. Today, France is a world leader in agriculture and tourism. It still has a reputation as a place of culture, with many talented filmmakers, fashion designers, artists, and writers working both at home and abroad.

▲ *France is considered a world leader in culture and the arts. The Louvre art gallery is one of the biggest tourist attractions in the country.*

Landscapes and Environment

French people refer to their country as L'Hexagone *because of its six-sided shape. As well as its land borders in the east and southwest, France is bordered by the English Channel, the Atlantic Ocean, and the Mediterranean Sea.*

Coastlines and Cliffs

There are around 2,100 miles (3,400 km) of coastline in France, including sandy beaches and white chalk cliffs. There is a spectacular coastline on the Mediterranean Sea, which is one reason why this area is a favorite spot for tourists from around the world. Corsica, the fourth largest island in the Mediterranean Sea, is also part of France.

PLACE IN THE WORLD

Total area: **211,210 sq miles (547,030 sq km)**

Percentage of world land area: **0.36%**

World ranking: **49th**

▼ *The coastal resort of Cassis in the south of France is famous for its cliffs and attracts visitors from all over the world.*

▲ *Mont Blanc lies in the Alps mountain range, on the border between France and Italy.*

IT'S A FACT!

France is home to the highest mountain in Europe, Mont Blanc (meaning "White Mountain"), which is 15,770 ft (4,807 m) above sea level. Monts du Cantal, in the Massif Central region of France, is the site of Europe's largest extinct volcano. It is nearly 50 miles (80 km) wide.

Farms and Forests

Large areas of low-lying, flat plains cover much of western and northern France. The weather here is mostly mild with regular rainfall, which makes it ideal for farming. Nearly one-third of French land is covered with forests, particularly in the hilly southern and eastern areas. There are more types of trees in French forests than in almost any other European country.

Mountains and Massifs

France is famous for its mountain ranges—the Alps, the Pyrenees, and the Jura—but one-sixth of the country is covered by an even older mountain upland called the Massif Central. Much of this vast region is covered in snow in winter, and peppered with extinct volcanoes.

▲ *The Loire Valley is one of the most beautiful regions of France, with picturesque villages and chateaus situated along the banks of the river.*

The Loire River

The Loire is the longest river in France. It flows north from the Massif Central to the Atlantic Ocean and covers a distance of 634 miles (1,020 km). During winter and spring the Loire often floods, which can cause damage to homes and farmland. In the summer, a lack of rain causes the water levels in the river to drop and droughts can be common, especially in hot southern areas.

Clean Energy

Around the world, countries are trying to balance the need for energy (for creating electricity, for example) with a desire to protect the environment. France gets some of its energy from hydroelectric dams along rivers such as the Loire and Rhône, and the electricity they produce is pollution-free. These dams reduce the problems of flooding and drought, but building them can damage natural habitats such as wetlands. Hydro-electricity will not run out, so it is called "renewable." France produces more renewable energy than any other country in the EU.

Nuclear Energy

Like many other countries, France uses nuclear energy. The country has 59 nuclear power plants, which provide 78 percent of all French electricity. In fact, so much electricity is generated that some of it is sold to other countries, making France the world's largest exporter of electricity. Despite the success of France's nuclear power program, it does have its problems. The radioactive waste produced when nuclear energy is generated is extremely dangerous, and it must be disposed of carefully. Nuclear power plants could also be targets for terrorists, so security is important.

GOING GLOBAL

When carbon fuels, such as oil, are burned, they produce carbon emissions that scientists believe contribute to climate change. Using nuclear energy has helped France keep its carbon emissions low, and now the country produces far lower levels of carbon emissions per person than most other industrialized nations. French electricity companies are now planning to build nuclear power plants in other countries.

▼ *The Cruas nuclear power plant lies on the Rhône River. It has four active nuclear reactors, providing around 5 percent of France's total energy supply.*

Population and Migration

Around 62 million people live in France, and another 2 million live in the French Dom-Toms. After World War II, the population of France grew dramatically, from 41 million to 51 million in just 20 years, but today the rate of population growth has slowed.

PLACE IN THE WORLD

Population: **64,057,792 (2009 est.)**

Percentage of world total: **0.92%**

World ranking: **22nd**

Young and Old

Since that period of fast population growth, the number of babies being born in France has dropped, and today most families have no more than two children. Like many European countries, France faces the problem of an aging population, and by 2030 there will probably be more elderly people (over 60) in France than younger ones (under 15).

◀ *These older men are playing the traditional French game of boules. Like many countries, France faces the problem of an aging population.*

▲ *The Fêtes de Bayonne is a festival held in the Basque town of Bayonne in August every year. Music and dancing are part of the festival, and the Spanish influence can be seen in events such as bull-running.*

The Basque People

The Basque Country is a region in southwest France that stretches into Spain. The people of the *Pays Basque*, as the French call it, have their own traditions and culture. For example, around one million Basques speak a unique language called Euskara—one of the oldest European languages—that is very different from either French or Spanish. Around 130,000 Basques live in France, but many more have moved to other parts of Europe or the U.S.

Long Lives

French people can expect to live for longer than most other Europeans. They also retire earlier, at the age of 60. This means that most elderly French people are able to enjoy 20 years or more of leisure time after they have stopped working. Their grown-up children have been called the "sandwich generation" because they are not only looking after their own children, but also their parents as they grow older and become frail or ill.

Searching for Work

Most people who live in France are of French nationality, but around 3.2 million are immigrants from other countries who have left their homes in search of work and better lives. There are around 550,000 Portuguese immigrants in France—more than any other single nationality. French people who leave the country to live elsewhere are called emigrants, and they are most likely to start new lives in Belgium, Germany, or Spain.

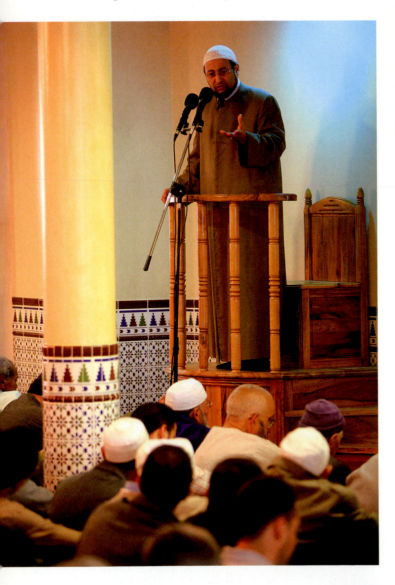

▼ *Many Muslims in France have come from North Africa. Here, the Moroccan imam Tareq Oubrou preaches in a mosque in Bordeaux.*

GOING GLOBAL

Nearly two million people live in the French Overseas Territories, or Dom-Toms:

French Guiana (northern South America): 209,000

Guadeloupe (Caribbean): 408,000

Martinique (Caribbean): 401,000

Réunion (southern Africa): 793,000

From Africa to Europe

The North African countries of Algeria, Tunisia, and Morocco have strong links to France, because they have all been ruled by the French in the past. Soldiers from these nations fought alongside French soldiers during World War I (1914–18), and after the war, many decided to stay in France. Since then, thousands of North Africans have traveled to France in search of work, and there are now more than one million North Africans living in the country.

▲ *French president Nicolas Sarkozy's parents were immigrants from Hungary and Greece, who came to France after World War II.*

Changing Places

Immigrants bring their skills, languages, and traditions to a country, and this can have a positive effect on society. In France, however, as in many other nations, immigration has also caused conflict with the local population, who worry that their lives may change as a result of the arrival of new people. Adjusting to a new country is also difficult for the immigrants. They may face problems with racism, and they may find it hard to get jobs without advanced skills, such as nursing or computing.

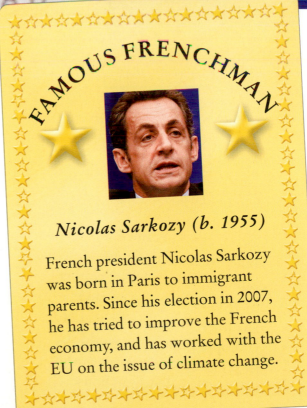

FAMOUS FRENCHMAN

Nicolas Sarkozy (b. 1955)

French president Nicolas Sarkozy was born in Paris to immigrant parents. Since his election in 2007, he has tried to improve the French economy, and has worked with the EU on the issue of climate change.

Culture and Lifestyles

French culture is famous all over the world. French food and clothes made in France are very popular in other countries. France has also been the home of many great artists, writers, and musicians.

France for Fashion

French fashion designers such as Coco Chanel, Christian Dior, and Yves Saint Laurent have influenced the clothing industry all over the world. Paris Fashion Week is held every year, and international clothes buyers visit the catwalk shows to see all the latest styles.

▲ *Paris Fashion Week attracts the biggest names from the global fashion industry. This model is wearing clothes by French designer Christian Dior.*

FAMOUS FRENCH WOMAN
Coco Chanel (1883–1971)

Coco Chanel became known in the 1920s for designing comfortable but elegant clothes for women. She also created perfumes, including Chanel No. 5. People all over the world still wear clothes and perfume made by the Chanel fashion house.

La Cuisine

The French call the art of preparing food *la cuisine*, and they take all aspects of food very seriously, from growing it to eating it. French food is regarded as among the best in the world, and is one of the most famous styles of cooking in Europe. There are more than 1,000 types of French cheese and, like many French food products, they are exported around the world. Countries in the Middle East buy more French food than any other region.

THE HOME OF...

Fine Food

The French's love for food has provided a number of dishes that are known worldwide:

Omelets: beaten eggs cooked with cheese, vegetables or meat

Quiche: an egg custard in a pastry crust

Boeuf Bourguignon: a beef casserole with red wine

Crêpes: thin pancakes, sweet or savory

Coq au Vin: chicken cooked with wine

A Global Culture

French culture has spread around the globe, especially in former colonies, such as the Canadian province of Quebec where many people speak both French and English. New Orleans is a city that was established by a Frenchman nearly 300 years ago. The effect of French culture is still felt in its annual Mardi Gras carnivals, in which enormous processions of dancers, musicians, and decorated floats create a party atmosphere that lasts for days.

▼ *The Mardi Gras celebrations in New Orleans reflect the city's French origins and culture.*

Growing up in France

Most French children enjoy a good standard of living, in comfortable homes with televisions, telephones, and washing machines. Education is free, and all children start school at the age of six, although many of them begin preschool when they are just three years old. Children have to stay in school until they are 16, but most of them choose to continue their studies beyond that age.

THE HOME OF...

The International Baccalaureate

When they are 16, French students can select courses that offer skills for work, or they can take the Baccalaureate—a qualification that allows students entry into higher education. There are more than 658,000 students worldwide who study the International Baccalaureate in 129 countries.

◀ Children in France can start school when they are three years old. Schools like this, for very young children, are called crèches or preschools.

Faith Matters

Around 85 percent of French people are Roman Catholics, but most of them do not go to church regularly. Islam is the second most common religion. The French state is described as secular, which means that religion is kept separate from areas such as politics and education. This has caused problems in schools when religious clothing, such as Islamic headscarves, has been banned. Some people say that they are being forced to choose between their right to an education and their religion.

A Passion for Sports

Soccer and cycling are two national passions that attract audiences from around the globe. The World Cup was proposed by a Frenchman, Jules Rimet, and was first held in 1930. When the tournament was held in France in 1998, the home team won. The Tour de France, which takes place in France every July, is the world's most famous cycling race and attracts around 20 teams of international riders each year. Thousands of spectators line the route to watch the race, which covers 2,235 miles (3,600 km).

IT STARTED HERE

Car Racing

Car racing began in France in 1894, when early cars raced between the cities of Paris and Rouen. These first road races were called Grand Prix, which means "great prize." These later developed into Formula 1 races, which are still known as Grand Prix.

▼ *The* Tour de France *is an international event, and millions of people around the world follow the cyclists' progress on TV and on the internet.*

Economy and Trade

France is regarded as one of the world's top six economic powers, along with the U.S., Japan, Germany, China, and the UK. After World War II, the French economy grew rapidly, increasing by up to 6 percent every year in a period that has become known in France as "the 30 years of glory."

◀ *In 2006, a law was introduced that said employers could dismiss people under the age of 26 from a job without having to give a reason. Thousands of young people protested against the law, and it was eventually changed.*

Finding Work

In 2006, the economy started to grow more slowly and the number of people without jobs increased, until by 2008 unemployment had reached around 7.8 percent. This problem affects young people in particular: around 20 percent of young people are unemployed —one of the worst rates of youth unemployment in Europe.

PLACE IN THE WORLD

Gross Domestic Product:
$2.866 trillion (2008 est.)

Percentage of world total: **2.3%**

World ranking: **5th**

Big Business

Since the 1970s, French industries have changed because manufacturers in other countries, especially in the Far East and Eastern Europe, began producing the same goods more cheaply. As a result, French businesses had to move away from heavy industries such as shipbuilding, to technology and services such as banking. Germany, Spain, the UK, and the U.S. are France's biggest customers of manufactured goods, which include machinery and vehicles.

Farming

France leads the rest of Europe in agriculture. Around 25 percent of French land can be used for farming or forestry, and France is responsible for 20 percent of all European agricultural products, such as cereals and wines. Most farmland is used to grow crops such as wheat and corn, and France is Europe's second leading producer of oilseed crops after Germany. Some of these crops are used to create biofuels, which replace imported fuels such as gas and diesel.

GLOBAL LEADER

Wine Production

France is famous for its fine wines, and it produces more wine than any other country—around 20 percent of the world total. However, people in France are drinking less wine now than they once did because of health concerns.

▼ *These people are harvesting grapes to be made into wine in the Fleurie region of France.*

▲ *The French TGV (Train à Grande Vitesse, or high-speed train) is the world's fastest passenger train.*

Links with Europe

France is one of 27 members of the European Union. By working together, the EU nations have created the world's biggest trading power, and the organization also provides aid—such as money and medical help—to less economically developed countries. Trading between EU members is helped by good transportation systems, and France has one of the busiest transportation systems in the world. Most goods in France are carried in trucks and semis, but trains, boats, and airplanes are also important methods of transportation.

IT STARTED HERE

Airbus

French, German, British, and Spanish companies worked together to build the world's largest passenger plane—the Airbus 380, which was launched in 2007. The consortium, known as European Airbus, is based in Toulouse, France.

Traveling by Rail

The fastest rail links in France can carry trains at speeds of 200 mph (320 km/h) from Paris to Strasbourg, making rail journeys to other European countries faster than ever before. Travel between France and the UK used to involve boat trips across the English Channel. It is still one of the busiest waterways in the world, but the number of ferries traveling in it has fallen since the Channel Tunnel was opened in 1994, enabling trains to travel beneath the sea.

Tourism

Around 80 million tourists visit France every year, with Paris and the Mediterranean coast being the most-visited places. In the summer, tourists flock to the coastal areas to enjoy the sun and sea. In the winter, most tourists visit mountainous areas to take part in sports such as skiing and snowboarding. Amusement parks have become more popular in recent years. Disneyland Paris attracts around 12 million visitors a year, making it one of Europe's top vacation destinations.

GLOBAL LEADER

Top Tourist Destination

France is the world's most-visited country, and it makes more money from tourism than any other country except the United States and Spain. It has 33 World Heritage Sites that have been recognized by UNESCO as places of global importance for culture or nature—more than either the United States or Russia.

▼ *Every year, thousands of tourists enjoy winter sports such as skiing in the French Alps.*

Government and Politics

France is a republic, which means that it is not ruled by a monarch, but by a prime minister and a president. As well as ruling its own people, the French government is very influential in world politics.

Two Houses

The French parliament is organized into two "houses," like Canada, and similar to the system in the United States. The lower house is called the National Assembly and its members are elected by the French people. The upper house is called the Senate. A prime minister leads the French government, but France also has a president who is chosen by the people in a separate election.

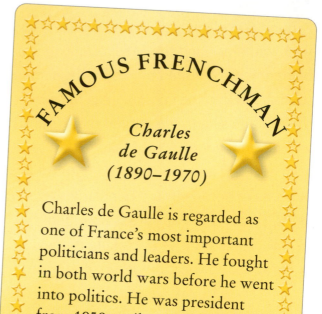

FAMOUS FRENCHMAN

Charles de Gaulle (1890–1970)

Charles de Gaulle is regarded as one of France's most important politicians and leaders. He fought in both world wars before he went into politics. He was president from 1958 until 1969, and during his period of leadership, most of the French colonies became independent states.

◄ *French politicians hold a debate in the National Assembly, the lower house in the French government. Representatives are chosen by the French people in an election.*

Power to the People

There are 22 *régions* in France, which give people a better opportunity to choose how they want their local areas to be governed. Each region has a council made up of elected members who control how money is raised, with local taxes, and then spent. They are responsible for the building of schools and public transportation systems and for helping local business people to trade.

IT STARTED HERE

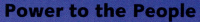

Revolution in Europe

Although the American Revolution took place in 1776, the effects of the French Revolution, in 1789, spread around the world, causing other revolutions to follow. The overthrow of the French king also began a chain of events that drew most of Europe into war. Thousands of men, women, and children—both rich and poor— were executed during the Revolution.

▶ *Gustave Eiffel designed the Eiffel Tower to celebrate the 100th anniversary of the French Revolution in 1889. The tower is 984 ft (300 m) high and was the world's tallest building when it was completed.*

The United Nations

France was just one of many countries involved in World War II, and when peace was restored in 1945, world leaders got together to create a new organization called the United Nations to prevent such terrible events from happening again. The UN now has 192 member states, including France, and UN soldiers may be called in to restore peace if wars break out. French troops have joined UN forces in Darfur, Liberia, and Lebanon, and have also worked in Afghanistan to try to bring stability to the troubled region.

Friends Across the Water

The UK and France have had an uneasy relationship over the centuries, with each nation having invaded the other as well as their colonies at different times in history. In 1904, the two countries agreed to create a "friendly agreement"—called the *Entente Cordiale*—that would create peace and cooperation between them. It was thanks to the *Entente Cordiale* that France and the UK were able to work together to end both world wars. Since then, the two countries have worked together in global affairs.

▼ *A family walks past French soldiers patrolling the road as part of their mission in Afghanistan in 2008.*

▲ *A doctor from Doctors Without Borders examines a man in a makeshift clinic in Kosovo in 2007.*

Doctors Without Borders

Doctors Without Borders (*Médecins sans Frontières*) is an international organization that brings emergency medical aid to places affected by war and natural disasters. It was established in 1971 by a group of French doctors and journalists. Today, doctors of many nationalities work for Doctors Without Borders, and it has brought medical aid to people in more than 80 countries. It was awarded the Nobel Peace Prize in 1999.

GOING GLOBAL

Francophonie is an international organization of countries where French is spoken and there is a strong French culture. There are more than 50 members of Francophonie, including Canada and Madagascar, which work together in the fields of economy, justice, and science.

The French have an expression, plus ça change, plus c'est la même chose, which means "the more things change, the more they stay the same." France may always be popular with tourists, and its food will always be admired, but French people will have to continue adapting to a rapidly changing world.

▼ *These people are taking part in a carnival in French Guiana, South America. Some people who live there would like more independence from French rule.*

Shrinking Influence

Some French Dom-Toms are already demanding independence from France, and more may try to separate themselves from the country by 2020. This could reduce the spread of French culture and language around the world. For example, English rather than French is considered the first language for business, so many former colonies could decide to introduce lessons in English or Chinese Mandarin in schools, so students will be able to communicate more easily with other people around the world.

Growing in Number

The world's population is growing, and it is expected to number around 7.5 billion people in 2020—an increase of 12 percent from the population of 6.7 billion in 2008. France will probably experience only a small increase in population, rising by just three percent, or two million people, by 2020. Around three out of every 2,000 people in France are immigrants, and that is not expected to change by 2020.

▼ *French president Nicolas Sarkozy shakes hands with Chinese president Hu Jintao. Improving relationships with growing economies such as China will be an important part of France's future.*

Facing the Future Together

The global economy is changing rapidly. Competing in the world's marketplace will be difficult for France, unless it joins forces with other European nations to create a new global power. In recent times, France has excelled in projects that have involved working closely with other nations—examples include building the Channel Tunnel and the Airbus 380, and advancements in the fields of medicine, research, and innovation. This is especially true of nuclear science, in which France is a world leader. When nations work together, they not only improve their economies, they also build a safer world for future generations.

Glossary

air resistance a force that slows down moving objects when they pass through the air.

biofuels fuels that are made from living things, especially from crops.

carbon emissions gases released into the atmosphere when fuels such as wood, oil, coal, and gasoline are burned. It is thought that these gases are contributing to climate change.

chateau large country houses or fortified palaces in France and French-speaking regions.

colony a country or a region that is under the political control of another country.

Dom-Tom a French Overseas Department or Territory.

drought a water shortage caused by a long spell of little or no rain.

economy the financial system of a country or region, including how much money is made from the production and sale of goods and services.

export to send or transport products or materials abroad for sale or trade.

hydroelectricity electricity that is generated using the power of falling or fast-moving water.

immigrant a person who has moved to another country to live.

import to bring in goods or materials from a foreign country for sale.

Islam a religion with belief in one god (Allah) and his last prophet, Muhammad.

monarch a king or queen.

Nobel Prize a prize given for outstanding work done in various fields, such as science, economics, and peace.

nuclear energy a type of energy generated by the splitting or joining of atoms.

racism the belief that all the people of a certain race have similar qualities and characteristics, and can be treated differently because of their race.

radioactive radioactive materials are unstable and produce radiation energy that can be very harmful.

tax a payment that must be paid to the government, often taken from a person's wage, or added to the cost of goods and services.

terrorists people who use violence or cause fear, to try and change a political system or policy.

wetland an area of marshy land.

Further Information

Books

The European Union Today
Simon Ponsford
Smart Apple Media, 2007

D-Day and the Liberation of France
Milestones in Modern World History
John C. Davenport
Chelsea House, 2009

Foods of France
Taste of Culture
Peggy J. Parks
KidHaven Press, 2006

France in Pictures
Visual Geography
Alison Behnke
Twenty-First Century Books, 2011

Life as an Immigrant
Understanding Immigration
Iris Teichmann
Smart Apple Media, 2007

Marie Curie: Mother of Modern Physics
Janice Borzendowski
Sterling Publications, 2009

Web Sites

http://us.franceguide.com
The official French Tourist Office site, with maps and information on France, its regions, and the Dom-Toms.

https://www.cia.gov/library/publications/the-world-factbook/index.html
Information and statistics on France.

http://www.socialstudiesforkids.com/subjects/economics.htm
Get to know economics with this site where topics such as money and trade are explained.

http://www.travelforkids.com/Funtodo/France/france.htm
Take a journey through France with this fun site, traveling from Paris to Provence.

http://europa.eu/youth
This European Union site has been set up especially for children and young people.

http://www.letscookfrench.com
This site has the recipes for some classic French dishes, including a selection of simple ones for children to follow.

Every effort has been made by the publisher to ensure that these web sites contain no inappropriate or offensive material. However, because of the nature of the Internet, it is impossible to guarantee that the contents of these sites will not be altered. We strongly advise that Internet access is supervised by a responsible adult.

Index

Numbers in **bold** indicate pictures.